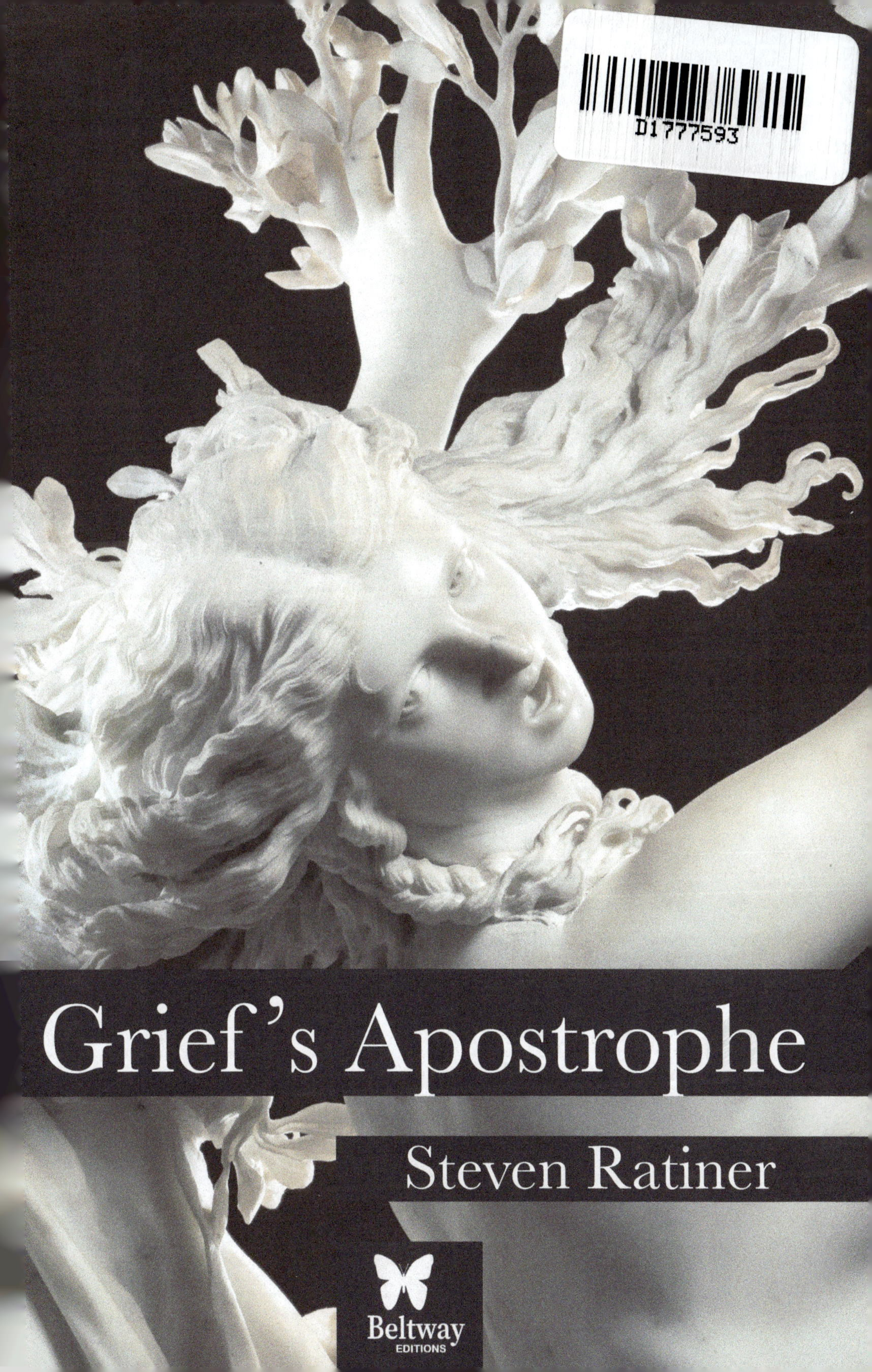

Grief's Apostrophe

Steven Ratiner

Beltway
EDITIONS

Grief's Apostrophe

Steven Ratiner

Beltway
EDITIONS

Copyright © 2025 Steven Ratiner
Edition Copyright © 2025 Beltway Editions

Published by Beltway Editions, 4810 Mercury Drive, Rockville, Maryland 20853. All Rights Reserved. No part of this book may be reproduced without the publisher's written permission, except for brief quotations in reviews. All rights reserved.

Printed in the United States of America

Cover Art: "Apollo and Daphne" by Gian Lorenzo Bernini, reproduced with the permission of The Galleria Borghese in Rome
Cover Design: Sara Cahill Marron
Author Photo: David Andrews
ISBN: 978-1-957372-17-4

Beltway Editions
www.beltwayeditions.com
4810 Mercury Drive
Rockville, MD 20853

Publishers:
Sara Cahill Marron
Indran Amirthanayagam

Acknowledgments

I'm grateful to the editors of these fine journals for first offering readers a chance to engage with these poems, and for permitting them to be reprinted in this volume:

Beltway Poetry Quarterly: "Citizen (Skeletal Villanelle #2)," "Anne" "Ballroom Dancing with the Bestial Dark," "Teatro Antico," "Clockwork," "Aeneas and Anchises," "Lettering," "Jews."

Blackbird: "Test," "Schubert (with the volume turned up)"

Hanging Loose: "Parocheth," "Learning the Business," "For Now," "Transcendental Postcard"

Ibbetson Street: "Sunday School," "Starbucks"

Parnassus: "Daughter"

Pedestal Magazine: "All Hallows," "Venetian Red"

Plume: "On the Corner of Bellington Street and Sparta," "Gott im Himmel," "Typos," "Burning Bush," "Said and Done"

Poet Lore: "Filial," "The Song"

Potlatch: "All the Time in the World"

QLRS (Quarterly Literary Review Singapore): "A Hunger," "A Text from Li Po," "Kigo"

Salamander: "The Arborist"

Solstice: "The Unveiling"

The Red Letters: "Supermoon," "Gold Boat," "Slainte," "A Soul"

The Writing Disorder: "She Loved"

"Clockwork" "Anne" "Typos" "Kigo" "Supermoon" and "*Slainte*" will appear in the anthology: *The Heart Off Guard: Poetry from Every Other Thursday*

"Supermoon" and "On the Corner of Bellington Street and Sparta" will appear in the *The Beehive Anthology*, Arlington, MA.

"What He Learned in the Locked Ward" will appear in the *Young Writers for Democratic Action* (Y-WDA) anthology *Truth*.

GRIEF'S APOSTROPHE

Contents

Typos   3

I

Clockwork   6
Fathering   8
Jews   9
A Hunger   10
The Corner of Bellington Street and Sparta   11
Test   12
Jack   13
Cat Skirl Steam Kettle Call to Prayer   14
Donning And Doffing   16
I Am Momentarily   17
For Now   18
Gott im Himmel   19
A Text from Li Po   20
Said and Done   21
Learning the Business   22
The Old Words   24
Bon Voyage   25
Parocheth   26
Kigo   27
Ballroom Dancing with the Bestial Dark   28

II

Pietà, Punctuated	32
The Burning Bush	33
O	34
What He Learned in the Locked Ward	35
Venetian Red	36
Selfie with God	37
Filial	38
Crib Fleece	39
"Drowned Syrian Toddler Washes Up On Turkish Resort Beach Near Bodrum"	40
Soft Target	41
A Conspiracy of Nouns	42
Teatro Antico	43
Citizen (Skeletal Villanelle #2)	44
Schubert (with the volume turned up)	45
Sunday School	46
King David	47
A Traditional Austrian Christmas	48
She Loved	50
All Hallows	51
Daughter	52
The Singer	53
Fold This Poem	54

III

Transcendental Postcard	58
Lettering	59
Visitation	60
Revising Paradise	61
The Unveiling	62
Anne	63

Aeneas and Anchises	64
What We Make	65
Sund	67
Greek Fragment	68
Provence	69
Oracle	70
Poem Beginning with a Line from Bob Hicok	71
The Arborist	72
The Song	74
From the Bridge	75
Gold Boat (The Broighter Hoard; County Derry)	76
A Soul	77
We	78
Carcinoma	79
Shadow Play	80
Apple	81
Escapement	82
Sabbath Rain	83
A Story about the Moth	84
Mending	85
Starbucks	86
Supermoon	87
Slainte	88
Grief's	89

There are many friends and colleagues—too many to list here—who deserve my thanks for generously supporting me and my writing, especially over the decade it took for the poems to grow into this collection. I cannot adequately express my gratitude for your caring, for your attention—but I hope you know what you mean to me.

MICHAEL NATHAN—who was, in almost every instance, the first reader for these individual poems; his decades of deep friendship and an unswerving faith in my work helped me through more dark days than I can remember, and often reminded me where the light was waiting.

DR. MATT CARMODY and DR. SUSAN ABELSON whose insights helped me more fully understand the fragility and resilience of the bodies and minds we each inhabit. My work, my ripening self, were certainly the beneficiary of their teaching.

THE EVERY OTHER THURSDAY POETRY GROUP whose clear-eyed attention to my poems—and broader commitment to the artform in all its complexity—helped my work to more-fully evolve. If a poem passed their discerning reading, I could be fairly confident it would be useful to others.

Poets MARTHA COLLINS and FRED MARCHANT —generous mentors and poetry bodhisattvas, whose limitless generosity has benefited so many in our writing community, myself included. They lit the fire under me that helped overcome inertia and fear, and then offered wise counsel in helping to shape this manuscript into its final form.

There are many other poet-friends who have inspired me by their own work while offering insightful commentary into mine. Three of the most essential: JANE HIRSHFIELD, TERESA CADER, DONALD HALL. Not just my poetry but my life is richer because of what we've shared.

The EDITORIAL TEAM at BELTWAY EDITIONS took great care in guiding my manuscript toward its final form, not to mention the refinement of its elegant design, and I will be forever grateful.

These poems are an homage to MY FAMILY and their abiding love, without which life quakes and meaning fails: devoted parents Anne and Abraham; my four sisters, living and gone; my son, daughter-in-law, and miraculous grandson, source of illimitable joy; and my far-flung extended family, who are my home without walls.

And for my wife KAREN—*my all and always*— whose love and wisdom defies description yet, without a doubt, can be found everywhere within these pages: THIS BOOK IS FOR YOU.

"All the new thinking is about loss.
In this it resembles all the old thinking."

—Robert Hass
"Meditation at Lagunitas"

Typos

Word instead of wood but,
sodden, it smoked when it burned.

I wrote god for good who was, once—
in my childhood years, crowned
with the nimbus of that capital G—
but now tends to be merely a placeholder
for nightmare, tears.

Seeking solace in the pastoral, but
grove came out as grave and the lymph nodes,
irradiated, naked as nymphs, danced
in a circle brandishing shovels while
nightjars, in downed pine, chanted
yis-gadal v'yis kadash sh'may raboh,
that dreadful trill—and all I could do
was stand there, heartless, composing
sorrow inside my head.

Glossolalia of the keyboard, my fingers
say what I cannot, never meant to, but
speak now nonetheless, because I am
marred by, married to this compulsive
language and cannot shut it (shout it) out,
even in this house of silence.

Live instead of love. Because that's
what's left for me without your yes—or
did I mean eyes?—to bless my brokenness.
Hello hell. These inked lines
sinking into white
cotton bond,
indelible.

I.

Clockwork

The dahlias are early this year.

A matter of days, they said.

The Perseid—stone-swarm, fist-sized, nickel-iron and silicate—
that comet's tail we pass through, regular as clockwork.

The hospice nurse arrives around noon.
Today, she's brought him a hot pastrami on seeded rye.
Not to eat, she explains—eating's out of the question—
just smell, just chew, then spit it into my hand.

One per minute, sometimes more.
Each bright arc. . .

In the eyes, in the ears,
in the tongue's lavish spill—this living.
And the pleasure I derived: to recognize, even now,
his boyish smile.

At four a.m., he explains, *before the sky's begun to lighten.*
Robins and blackbirds. Then mockingbirds,
mourning doves, warblers, chickadees.
A lull, sometimes. But then the cardinal's
brazen aria. Cacophony, I ask him?
Shifting uneasily in the bed, pain creasing his brow:
ecstasy.

The aching. The waiting.

A matter of hours.
Windows streaked with pollen,
sun making his rounds.

The E-train to Jamaica, transferring to
the Q-5 bus and the slow crawl along Merrick, then
a three-block walk up Francis Lewis.

In my chest, opening like a dahlia,
this nova of white petals,
edged with violet and gold.

Like clockwork. Like fate.

A matter of minutes. Late.

Fathering

After the stroke, when language
froze over in his throat, he had a hard time

with the snow—   He couldn't say,
and the sky wouldn't stop saying—

We went walking, and the tracks
in our wake—   And the cardinal-

red calligraphy scribbled between trees—
And the ticking like Morse across hat brim—

And the time I was certain his hiss
was about to coalesce into *Steven*—

And the dream I kept having: moon-
slick trail rising between birch ribs, breath

becoming smoke, ink becoming breath—
Writing these words across the page—

And even before the sentence is complete,
the footprints filling up with white—

Jews

"Jews," says my mother, out of nowhere,
at the kitchen table, staring off at—what?
The next door neighbors? The garden feeder?
Our own reflections? Agreeing, I tell her,
the chickadees wear black *yarmulkes*.
"And the waxwings,"—her sly smile—"they wrap
their prayer shawls smooth across those bony shoulders
like your grandfather did, remember?" I nod.
What to say, then, concerning the sparrows
scattering millet? And the mourning doves
chanting *Elohanu*, gleaning in the bleached grass?
Is sunshine and abundant seed, perhaps, a vision
of the Promised Land? And the blue jay's *shofar*,
the call to prayer for a feathered diaspora?
Now my mother gazes upward through
the dogwood canopy where a jet liner's bright sliver
points like a *yad*—blue scripture unscrolling
across our September morning. Like a child reading,
her lips move. Though I don't know it then,
this is the last time my mother will ever visit my home.
I put up a second pot of coffee, toast the corn muffins.
Light cream. Her packets of Splenda. The quiet
between us. I lay my palm across the cobbled streets
of old Jerusalem—my mother's arthritic hand.
"Amen" she murmurs, as if no one is listening.

Hunger

When she was six her father taught her
innocence: how the eyes must empty and her face
go placid as Dongting Lake in the old pictures and songs.
Then, drifting through the bird market, she could
snatch a duckling or a dove, snap its neck
and sweep it beneath her skirt, all in one motion.
Don't think, he'd tell her. *Don't even imagine*
the tender flesh slipping from slender bones.

Guizhou, thirty years and half a world behind her.
Now, some mornings she'll wake in the quiet house,
and feel the wet between her legs, red droplets
berrying the white sheets. She skips breakfast
to catch the Concord Ave. bus to Fresh Pond where
she can walk the wide path around the reservoir, her eyes
crossing and re-crossing the great expanse, trawling
a hunger so deep, it swallows memory, swallows even
this lustrous April sky. It leaves her with little more
than the old song they sang, squatting there with her father
under pin-prick stars, pine twigs spitting into darkness,
still waiting for the black pot to boil.

The Corner of Bellington Street and Sparta

What could be more seemly?
To have three strong sons dress you,
in breast plate and greaves, raising you up
on your shield, carrying you downstairs
to the minivan where we can all
drive up to Farnhams' for fried clams,
and then perhaps the boardwalk above Crane's,
to watch the brute surf slash and parry,
lunge and retreat, the comely maidens
ditching school and the boys stretched out
across their polished boards as if they were
the prows of dragon ships, venturing out
and returning in triumph—and so I say goddamn
to the doctors and their blood-work oracles,
goddamn to the festering pancreas, goddamn
to the clamor of battle no longer needing
my strong arms, my courage.
And curse as well the wintery god Metastasis,
all the bloody spoils amassed in His keep,
and what care I if the mechanical bed is my
paltry throne and if, in a week, coma
like an invading army will overwhelm
my defenses and claim my vast lands? Who
can say I have not earned my sovereign sleep?

Test

Dutiful is to *filial* as:

mournful is to *tearful*;

awful is to *forgetful*;

fearful is to *blood-*
      rimmed bitten-down cuticles, the throbbing
      pain its own peculiar balm;

or, *hateful* is to *shameful*, my mother's
      failing body (*the body I am heir to*),
      the blighted protein making lace
      of her beleaguered brain, making off with
      half my life in the process, and damning me to
      dread the remainder of these fissured days
      the old Greeks would have branded *fate*
      but today is simply the *matter-of-fact*
      braided-noose of genetics and luck.

Hurtful root-bound with *grateful*.
Armful cradled into *spadeful* almost overnight.
To curse one's own breath is neither
brave nor fiercely honest. Love's void
and death's are not analogous.

Jack

Little Lamb who made thee?

When the surgeon began to resect the bowel,
he found them scattered all through the folds

of the haustra like stiff-fleeced sheep
in December fields, huddling in the lee

of hillock or fence, the season too advanced
for resistance. He sutured up my stepfather

and, that evening, when Jack's mind cleared,
explained with a studied calm there was

"nothing to be done." From the monitor,
the little green trochees of heartbeat.

Dost thou know who made thee?

Cat Skirl Steam Kettle Call to Prayer

Dopplered by distance, the muezzin of a siren.

Bee chant from delphinium minaret.

Robins davening on the lawn,
bowing to bless each white grub unearthed.

Next door, Miles spilling
from a bedroom window, *Blue*, side one.
Kitty-corner, Basset Hound and skill saw
trading eights.

The kyrie of dog-day cicadas.

The sweet measures of mown grass,
home-going traffic, my own breath.

As it turned the corner, the din of the ambulance
commanding all attention.

Carrying him out—so bundled on the gurney,
he could barely offer us a nod, a weak smile.
Standing across Bellington. Nothing to be done.
We nod in return.

Only when the siren drains away
do I hear the frantic kettle.

For a time, I do not sip but only
breathe in the steaming jasmine,
feel how it wets the eyelids, nostrils,
the grotto of each breath.

Donning and Doffing

The procedure.
What they taught us in nursing school.
The PPE in sealed bags.
Cap, gown, gloves, mask, face shield of
molded acrylic—a defense against
the microscopic castaways of virus adrift
on even a patient's shallow breath, or settled
on cheeks pale as moon-blanched sand.
And only then, after suiting up, am I free
to attend them: Mrs. R and Mr. L in the isolation ward,
walled off from family and friends, consumed by
the slow process of dying alone.
They too must follow procedure and,
one by one, remove all the soul's familiar apparel—
gown, gloves, mask of the weary self,
cap of the given name—until what remains is
merely human. And then, beneath white fluorescence,
and with or without my aid, even the knotted ribbon
of a final breath can be undone.

I Am Momentarily

all the people you believe
me to be: the other daughter,
buried sister, childhood
row house friend, and then
the good-looking boy who
fissured your mill town heart,
the heart you held me to
a hundred lifetimes ago.
I am guest at the beginning of a rant,
then suspect stranger at the end where you
introduce yourself again, and again,
asking whether I work here.
I smell gardenias, onion, urine.
You rebuff my hand.
Another hallway castoff,
I'm at a loss for words.
This morning, we become mother
and daughter again—if momentarily,
and in someone's half-
remembered story. Together, we are
the prodigal and the welcome home.
We may even be the fatted calf
ablaze on the spit, and the murmured
gratitude to celebrate our
very next forgetting.

For Now

Near the end, she stopped
eating altogether. One evening,
when I brought chicken soup shoaled
with wild rice, a quick shake of her head,
whispering: *what for?* And yet, in sleep,
her mouth moved constantly, making a meal
of departure. Watching her, I wondered:
was the opposite of hunger *grief? Grace?*
Love or *need* —what feeds on our silence?
Not that it would have made a difference,
but I wish I'd proposed we take turns
with the spoon, a mouthful, a mouthful,
countering *what for* with *for now*.

Gott im Himmel

Gott was thicket, thorned, glottal,
a vine knotted inside my grandmother's throat.

im's pressed lips implied opening, a threshold,
vibration, promise, dispensation.

Himmel channeled sun into my ears, hills
upon fabled green hills, breath-trill, arrival.

Her hovering gaze. My fingertip tracing the maze
of her furrowed cheek. Pearl-gray-cloud-tremor: those eyes.

Remembering our days. How I mouthed syllables as if
I'd understood. Understanding nothing: my blessing in disguise.

A Text from Li Po

Li Po woke at three a.m. believing
the moonlight, spilled at the foot of his bed,

was snow—that snow meant mountains, home,
ink-soaked skies, and the way his mother's voice

made morning of his name. A thousand years
and the Chinese repeat it still: same poem, same

untethered gaze, same mother, home, un-
embraceable moonlight melting into reed mats like

a dusting of snow. Three a.m., and I woke this morning
with a brushstroke of moonlight across the blue

carpet beside my bed. I mistook it for
Chinese poetry. But it was only the sound of

a thousand years laughing softly. So:
write something down in that damned

notebook of yours; sip your tea slowly;
and phone your mother.

Said and Done

So angry I could spit.

Something old people said but they didn't mean it.

I heard them on the front walk in a bubble of streetlight and I peeked
    from my bedroom window.

My uncle, in a gray stripy suit, explaining, and flapping his hands
    as he talked while

Momma folded her arms across her chest and stared daggers.

Only bits and pieces: "savings. . .insurance," and then with a screech
I'd never heard gush from Momma's throat—

"from your own brother's widow!"

If this were a cartoon, he'd have shrunk inside his clothes and run away
    buck-naked. But he didn't run,
he reached out his hand. Something was in it. And right then I saw
    my mother
spit on the ground where he stood. His black shoes shiny in the light.

Learning the Business

Come Saturday, when the steel vats backed up,
you were the one, Daddy, who answered the call,

drove down Jamaica Ave., stripped to the waist,
and fished two hundred pounds of dry cleaning

from the murky slosh, gabardine dresses and
suit coats laid out across the work bench like

the bodies of the drowned. Find the clog,
flush the line, rescue the day, get the crew

back to work—while somewhere your father
sat chanting in temple; your brothers, boisterous,

at Sardi's or the track. I remember you bought me
an ice cream and I perched on a high stool, watched

as you half-disappeared into the benzene tank, licking
my vanilla swirl, giddy with the fumes.

Driving home you told me, when I was older,
you'd teach me the business, how to keep the books,

so I'd have nothing to do with the scald of the six-
foot presses or the chemical brew. Sixty years later,

and here, Daddy, I'm making my accounting:
your left hand knuckled on the steering wheel;

your right idly strumming the cords of my neck;
and me, wedged beside you, mouth slack with sugared milk.

These days, I read neither ledger nor prayer book—
but remember this: you were two-hundred pounds that

Saturday morning; a little more than half that when,
come January, the orderlies wheeled you back

from radiation on the steel gurney, laid you
into your hospital bed limp as laundry.

The Old Words

The hole of it. The dirt of it.
The wet seep. The deepening dark.
The half-lit, head-first, half-gone.
The red-clay-veined cold cradle.
The dampening sounds.
The stiff canvas bundle smeared with tar.
The thrum of the old words, repeating.
The stubborn drumming of the heart.
The blackened hands. The tamped mound.
The ache of the spine uncoiling.
The going, and then the going on.
The forever-knowing what is up
by never forgetting what is down.

Bon Voyage

My dear passenger.
Breath's your passport, blue
and red official seals, all borders
swinging open to you.
Sky's flagship boarding. And white
against the white of the pillowcase,
your face, the flag's emblem:
a starveling eagle, a rippling mirage.
Listen now: the thrumming of turbines,
whitecaps ebbing on the heart monitor,
blood's tidal *bon voyage*.

The mooring lines are released.
Suddenly, I find myself standing
alone on the pier, waving madly.
Can you still see me? Smile, please,
wave back one more time. The alarm—
startling as a ship's horn, it declares:
no harbor can hold me now.
The nurses come rushing in on their rubber-
soled shoes, auraed by fluorescent sun—
so determined, they run straight through
the fog-bank I've become.

Parocheth

Her rasping breath,
embroidered by silence.

Blue moons at the fingertips.
Grizzled early morning light.

We prepared ourselves and were
wholly unprepared. The moment

the curtain was drawn back,
our tears unscrolling—this:

what remained of the covenant,
nearly weightless in our arms.

Kigo

Crow, searching for a branch
in an autumn poem, finds
this winter memory instead.
Mist, escaped from some spring verse,
drifts across my snowed-in garden.
Rice paper unscrolling,
and the smell of fresh-ground ink.
I make *moon* and the hooked stroke
fishes up your half-forgotten face.
I must have been eight, couldn't sleep.
Even late, the derision of crows from
our neighbor's pine, a child's portent.
I called and you came to me, sitting
for a moment on the edge of my bed,
wicking away my fears when
you could do nothing about your own.
Your gauzy nightgown, like the moon's—
The way you both looked down.
A pity, time waters memory's ink.
Words bleed through the *kozo*. Still,
perhaps a new poem will come from this:
tears, the *kigo* —emptiness, the season.

Ballroom Dancing with the Bestial Dark

Emptiness: encircling my waist, clasping
my cold palm, drawing me close—the fox-

trot, the clawed waltz, the lunge-
feint-retreat, into and out of our most

private spaces, wind-combed fur cha-cha-cha.
And her feral perfume: rain, rot, iron

in the blood, terror's pheromones,
the clinking of our canines, the knot

of wet tongues. Raspy breath now,
head falling back, hair almost sweeping

sky's polished expanse, I'm death's
wallflower no more, gliding across this moon-

lit ballroom—minus, suddenly, the music,
moon, partner, and even the feel of the floor.

II.

Pietà, Punctuated

It seemed to her only minutes between open
parentheses gazing down lovingly comma
bud of the child's mouth working ceaselessly

comma of colostrum wetting the chin em
dash and now the mother's eyes emptied and
flushed with tears comma again looking down as

this chasm of grief opens across her lap ellipses
like entry wounds still bleeding period closed
parentheses swinging shut like the door of a tomb.

The Burning Bush

I pretend not to listen, tell myself
I'm just out for the June of it,
an excursion, the effort of the climb.
I observe buds on the wild lavender,
ammonites in the fissured granite.
In my world, everything burns—
faces, skies, grand cities, the reservoir
of human memory—so how worked up
need I become over one nettled scrub
aflame. . .and fluent. . .and addressing me
by my father's father's name?

O

Interred within a single character:

O, gaveled inside the brain—
indelible as the keystroke of a typewriter.

O, the black corona encircling the moon,
loitering outside the hospice window,
one day shy of full.

O, your pale lips in sleep
feigning astonishment.

O, immobilized, the hours, the days—
soap bubbles popping.

O, the curt in-rush of breath
when I knew it was over— and

O, the slow exhalation, thinking:
what now? what now?

O, the bright urn containing what could
not depart as smoke.

Each morning, waking beside
the framed black-and-white.
And even now nettled by the unasked questions.
O, your one syllable elegy:

O, Mother. If only.

What He Learned in the Locked Ward

In the asylum, he explains, we were
a fellowship of those who could no longer
lift our end of the coffin, the ungainly weight,
brute gravity, too much for our thinning arms.
We'd hoist nothing heavier than
lithium in a paper cup, or the granite
hours we quarried after lights-out.
And the pain we each bore was the knowledge
that the world carried on unchanged without us,
more than enough on hand to steady the casket,
shovel the hole, tamp the turned earth.

Venetian Red
    —for Michael Nathan

In the dream muddle, lolling
across mama's lap, the blue-gray
of her unwavering gaze—and just beyond,
the gibbous moon, a yellow birch leaf
still on black water, then—late!
Tower bells clanging and so
we're off, my companions in tow, racing
through shadowy streets cobbled with
eyes, teeth, blue veining the ancient city.
"Sola, perduta, abbandonata…"—a gondola
gliding past, the aria surging with each
thrust of the boatman. *"E nel profondo
deserto io cado…"*—the toothy smile
of a death's head sideways on the prow.
Lost, I stop an old woman, asking *a la ferovia?*—
but she sends us here instead: foundry,
furnaces belching red, ingots
of pig iron and bone. *Getto*
becomes *gâteau*, the Duchess with
red encrusted lips, hair moussed
in black flame and every forkful
she raises stares back, bears a name.
"But for you, *miei bambini*:" (with a flourish,
voice like crushed glass), *"panetti!"*—the oven
crammed with little loaves browning in their tin beds.
From there it's only a half-step to
pietà, mother's stone lap, and my head rocks back,
limp arm a pendulum, every lost second
another thorn—and just like that all my dreams
draft up the sooty chimney, tear-smoke
like an oily mist staining the terracotta roofs,
the gilded domes, even God's hovering
moon-bleached hosts.

Selfie with God

He moved. Thus the blur. Thus the fray
of violet cloud scarfing the icy peak.
His eyes: no, not there, those are
geese, or blown leaves or.
But I'm clear as can be. My un-
canny smile, confident that over
my right shoulder, gazing down:
He. More autumnal light. More or.
An etherful. All the bliss of His thus.
And after all, isn't that
His nature, His strength?
He moves, unerringly. While I hold Him
at arm's length.

Filial

Isaac is carrying his father's
bones in a brown paper bag,
slow up the brick steps, pausing,
key wavering before the slim
black cleft, pausing again, shouldering
the oak door open, nudging the switch,
amber light spilling from twin sconces
onto the shrine of the familiar—his parents'
couch, sideboard, cherrywood credenza,
each in its own unbroken skin—
then shuffling into the kitchen, the drone
of the Frigidaire, the stove's dim moon—
before setting the sack down on the counter
and removing, one by one:
corn meal, lamb shank, ripe tomato,
black bread, and a knuckled clove of garlic.

Crib Fleece

The Lord is my shepherd and so
I ate, shat, fattened in green pastures,
rutted on spring mornings, bleated my praise.
In late spring I begat, nursed, led
my clamoring drift out to grassy slopes,
slowly forgot the feel of warm mouths
pulling at the teat. Wind swept across the days,
until the season was complete and,
in chilly gusts, I rose up, dangling
from a red hook above the world,
and wept.

"Drowned Syrian Toddler Washes Up On Turkish Resort Beach Near Bodrum"

1.
It looks as if he's listening.
Ear pressed against wet sand, this
three-year-old Odysseus:
What sings—and why does it hold me?
What, beneath sea, beneath earth, and why
wasn't I told? Where
were they bringing me? Who
will I be once I get there?

This is where the Aegean left him—
red tee unveiling the swollen belly,
sodden blue shorts and battered knees.
What should have been school shoes
will crack now and bleach from brine and sun.
Already, a salt halo drying atop his crown.

2.
Half-listening to the evening news—
latest war, latest disaster, refugees
swept from one misery to another,
as regular as the tides. Did I just
mishear the reporter's question:
Whose child *isn't* this?

Soft Target

In our classroom, an abacus
of bullet holes upon which they learn

addition (the sum of wild screams)
and subtraction (the screams falling silent.)

In this new blood curriculum—
and with alarm bells clanging—

first graders are schooled in last words,
the show-and-tell of open wounds,

how to relinquish every loved thing,
singing *ashes, ashes, we all fall down.*

Now all the feathery doors fly open.
Recess is endless. *A my name is Alice*

and my mother's name is Anguish—
hovering, mid-air, within an empty ellipsis.

Such elegant penmanship, inscribed
across a sheet of polished granite.

A Conspiracy Of Nouns

A cake of soap.

A skein of accusations.

A bevy of mass arrests.

A gaggle of horrors.

A doily of flayed skin.

A bouquet of agonizing cries.

A string of pearl-white eyes in
the dark of a makeshift dungeon
three floors beneath the old courthouse.

A cornucopia of outright lies which
the newspapers copy down, print verbatim.

A spasm of spoken names
rising like sparks from the husk of their sleep:
Amira, Fiona, Joseph, Jafari, Li Jing, Maria—
and, of course, the continual refrain of
Mama, Mama, Mama.

A cake of soap.

A cascade of silences pooling
in a shaded glen where the mind retreats
from cold porcelain, but only so often.

Washing the body.

A rosary of bubbles circling the drain.

Teatro Antico

Noon in Siracusa.
Sun-fissured stone tiers.
Rosefinch lights on the steps,
my Aeschylus, his blood-washed face.
Cloud-scud and dry winds through hilltop olive,
our murmuring chorus. Alone here, I am fate, I am audience—
me, and all the insatiable kings I carry within, all the blind fathers
who squander their progeny like spilt wine—so the stingy gods might
bless their fruitless wars, their bountiful carnage—all
for a remembered face, a stolen strand of beauty,
never ours in the first place.

Citizen (Skeletal Villanelle #2)

Unbear-
able, this white erasure,
our snow-blighted nowhere.

As if we were
evicted from our very
skins, given one bare

room in this barbed wire
subdivision, tenants-at-will
in Rancho Nowhere,

nothing but vacancies, despair
by the week or the month,
whatever the market will bear.

Front door. Frontier.
Refugees whose passports
are stamped *Nowhere*,

No One, with neither flag nor
homeland. "Show some gratitude,"
the gold-barred lapel pin through bare
flesh: *"Citizen Nowhere."*

Schubert (with the volume turned up)

Measure after measure.
Lieder strung with barbed wire.

∂

At this volume, the speakers tremble.

The German tenor, his voice
like ripened fruit with
the rot gouged out.

∂

Too much grave in this *Ave*.
More despair than grace in her *Maria*.

∂

*On such an exquisite morning how could one
do anything but sing? Spring-stirred hillsides,
cloud upon cloud like heaven's battlements,
even the columns of smoke quickly dispersed
by a southerly breeze.*

∂

Immeasurable.
All those hollow black eyes gazing out
between the taut black staves.

Sunday School

*God moved across the face
of the waters* as her arm swung
wide across the blackboard
across the face of pale cloud
of chalk dust raining like silence,
and *the earth was void* and I
was v*oid and without form.*
We'd copied the verse *the face
of the deep* into our blue-
lined notebooks, our minds
void and bored by the pinched
holiness in her voice—but
I remember her slim arm and
how, beneath the rayon bodice,
God moved across a watery swell
and then, without warning, *the void*
took shape and thrust upward and
I was awed by possibility, the molten
surge like a new verse being born and
even my *God* quick breath stroking
the heavenly *face of the waters* was
like music, like Genesis, and all
came *holy* into existence, the word
moved possessed form and *was good*.

King David

wielded both harp and sword, and guess
which did the most damage? Which
one's flourish yielded the most tears?

As sovereign, he could make love his guest,
conscripting the loyal husband for a sandy ditch
beside a battlefield. (Psalms have tongues but no ears.)

Between rivers, between a woman's legs: the surplus
by which kingdoms flourish and kings touch
history's bloody hem. The old gods are buried here.

A Traditional Austrian Christmas

1.
Did I dream this?
Schlaf in himmlischer Ruh!
Curlicues of chimney smoke.
An Advent calendar shaped like a line
of cattle cars. For each of twenty-five nights,
one door slides back and a new flock
of cooped-up souls is swept into darkness.

2.
When Grandpa sang *Stille Nacht,* I thought it meant
Night Made Out of Steel. Something molten in his voice.
His schnapps and corrugated smile. *Ssh!* he whispered,
don't tell Grandma. We all knew:
chocolates in his sweater pocket and,
in his sock drawer, a black-sheathed bayonet.

3.
*I can always smell one, anywhere
in the building.* Grandpa made a poopy face.
Goldschmidt in 3-B. Cabbage boiling in vinegar.

4.
A Comice pear swaddled in gold foil as if
it were the Christ Child. Salvation: *when it's ripe,
you can eat it with a spoon.* I to XXV:
I drew the old numerals like black spears.
Does that make me a little bit Roman?
The soup pot made Grandma's glasses weep.

It is finished. The murmur of my empty stomach.
Lacking a spear, will a steak knife do?
We were stewed in such theology: *God's love*
so tender, it falls from the bone.

She Loved

She loved the way *(love you)* he swallowed
when he said it.

Swelling in his palms, her breasts
had palms of their own, begging for each
pinched copper of desire.

She savored the way his blind tongue
ventured out, reading and re-reading
the Braille apostrophe—his mouth, savory
with scotch, smoke, salt, want.

The waul of gasped syllables.
She learned to love the vast unsaying
their love became.

Nearing the end, pleasure turned her
inside out—and all the tenderest tissues,
pinking with bliss and oblivion,
were exposed to the world—while
all the sweet scarred burden
of his body grew weightless and found,
at last, a respite within.

All Hallows

We gut the pumpkins—the ones
we let our children pick from
the long rows of a parking lot
decked out like a farmer's field.
We even let our preschoolers
handle the knives, one to hack
a gap-toothed grimace, one to gouge
the smirk from startled eyes.
Then we dress them up as all
the monstrous and abortive selves we
feared we might become—or all
the pink-cheeked, princely dreams
we feared we'd never. After dark,
we send them out in packs and
every front door swings open before them,
tribute heaped in their paper sacks.
Chocolate is their God. *Pretend*
is how they worship Him. Later that night,
while the children sleep, we steal
Milky Ways from their hoard, Hersheys
and Almond Joys. All the treats
doled out sparingly when we were young—
there's no one to stop us now. And yet
we let each mouthful loll on the tongue,
to make the pleasure last. Finally, the ritual:
door to door, securing this handsome fortress
from whatever waits beyond. A Chivas
on the rocks and, masquerading as our parents,
we make love on the couch with the TV on—
as if we didn't hear the bloodless wind trying
all the door locks and window sashes, as if
we still desired every bit of this life as much
as we do the milk, the dark, the bittersweet.

Daughter

"That little face. . ."
He told me it was like
his wife's roses, surrendering
color so slowly they
barely noticed until the morning
the blanched petals lay
scattered beneath the vase.

They brought roses to the hospital
hoping the familiar smell would
remind her, coax her return.
In the silent room,
the plunge and hiss of the breathing machine.
The legato of late afternoon sun.

The coma was interminable, almost
a rehearsal for death. "Or maybe," he said,
"she's just allowing us time. . ."—
the voice trailing as the thought unwinds.
As for the girl, it was only a comma
in a brief declarative sentence,
the sort a seven-year-old
would pen in wobbly hand,
with that squat and careless period,
like a new moon, floating at the end.

The Singer

"Though the rain it raineth every day."
—King Lear

And the sun it sunneth on good days and bad,
while the pain it paineth the deserving and the un-.

Joy, too, it joys—but fickle and rare—
while death is sheer diligence, at palace and byre.

When dreams are furrowed so deep in the earth,
who knows what seed continues its growth.

So I dip my pen into every knowing well—
with a hey, ho, the wind and the rain—

though the troubled ink bleeds through,
page after page, and only death is indelible.

So what good my song if there's no heart to sing it,
and no ear to carry it back into sunlight?

Yet the rain it calmeth a poor poet's pain—
and the song sings still within the strumming rain.

Fold This Poem
—*for Gene Vroom*

in half lengthwise, then bring the corners
to meet the center line, crease sharply, and again,

bowing inward from the margins to form
the swept-back wings that conjure lift, loft,

a reprieve from gravity. Know, please,
how much cargo I've secured within

this paper's hold—and yet how very-
nearly weightless it is, my joy, my grief.

Assuming you've read the poem once, twice,
whatever scrutiny paper wings will bear—

then wait, please, no longer:
grasp this contrivance in a raised hand,

draw back, and hurl it like a spear,
watch it swoop and veer, negotiating space—

the glide, the grace, and eventual fall.
Notice too, if you will, the feel

of your open hand, and the now-
emptied air, your own unpleated longing,

your as-of-yet unwritten *now?*

III.

Transcendental Postcard

Wish you were. Here,
the downpour has let up
and sail blades divide
one blue from another.
The eye bathes in light's
sheer indifference.
Like carved figureheads,
bearded iguanas stare out from
the smooth limbs of the turpentine.
This whole island is a prow
rocking at anchor. You'd
have loved this blue stillness.
I'd have loved any weather
which delayed your departure.

Lettering

1.
I've only a few of them, my mother's letters.

How her shapely script leans West, each capital
proud, like the gnomon of a sundial whose
lengthening shadow—whose dwindling hours—
whose dire half-past—whose longed-for quarter-to—

2.
All morning, the sky a parchment-gray.

I've no letters at all from my father—
only this *Hamsa* dangling from its silver chain.
What a fine hand emptiness has, the blue-black
indelible silence.

Visitation

Your voice—not the whole of it,
just a wounded vowel—racing past,
inches above my bare head, then
sweeping up to perch on a third-
floor iron rail, preening, a roil
of snowy feathers in November wind.
If not for reflex, it might have
gored me right between the eyes—
the first line of this poem, *your voice*—
owl-taloned, remembrance, the shrift
of evening light—not the whole force
of your absence, but enough.

Revising Paradise

Cloud-scroll. The spell of it.

Blue-black verses spackled with red marks.
~~his~~ will (atop *its*^ three-stroke pedestal):
a gradual perfection. Am I still uncorrected?

Here, the tiny peaks of carets—each summit,
an aerie for some new seraphic voice.

And there, the inexorable bar of deletion,
trailing off like a curl of smoke. It sends
questionable angels plummeting into darkness.

Like childhood, I am held between
invisible margins. Everywhere, pilcrows
like the pillars of a child-sized temple. *His* pen,
enshrined upon the altar. And inscribed above:

The Author is never seen, never not seen.

Uncomforted, I cling to my bafflements.
My *longing* feels italicized. Parentheses, arching
above my head and below, to close ranks with the blessed.
But between one radiance and the next, I can't help
scanning the crowds for my pantheon of faces,
for love's emendations. . .

What good would ellipses be without them?

The Unveiling

Rain skinning granite.

I lay the flat of my palm, let
pools gather between fingers,

streams skim the blue veins down.

This is the real, I know it—
stone, rain, blood, December cold—

the irresistible claim of the material.

And then there's you, love—or rather
the absence of you—how the morning,

gored by your departure, healed

without a scar, emptied even
the watery syllables of your name,

cut deep into polished black stone.

Here, my hand reaching—and there
my own hand reaching back.

Anne

My mother took their names—it's what
a woman did then—the bonds of marriage, more
honor than ownership: Ratiner, Silverstone, Rich.
Three *beloveds* and, after time, her steadfast hands
helped nurse each into darkness—what a woman did—
until, alone again, it came her turn to wed
oblivion. The dowry of molecules.
The infinitesimal bursts of energy, bonds
breaking, joining again, the earth's
bacterial vow: *I do, I do.* A hundred years
since your birth, Mother, and this rain-
tilled April morning I woke up wondering
what I should call you now:
Anne Carbon, Anne Nitrogen,
Mrs. Silence.

Aeneas and Anchises

Behind us, the white towers burned.
Frenzy of blood, and the cries
of the dying. I carried you, Father,
on my back, along the rocky path
from Troy to Ithaca, turning south to
Flatbush and then Queens—where the rot
of your own father's dry cleaning plant
lay siege to your dreams—
and the benzene fumes, sharp as spears,
split your breastplate and did, in the end,
what the Greeks could not.

Still, I went on carrying you,
into the citadels of academia,
through airports and hill towns,
indifferent crowds, contentious solitude,
and across page upon page of heartsick stanzas
marching like the ranks of Achaeans.
My poor father, skein of bones and whispers,
even now, draped across my bent back
like a prayer shawl—though, to the crowds
lurching behind me up 9th Ave.,
all they'll notice is my sweat-stained collar,
the scruff of my sun-scorched neck.

What We Make

1.   *Naiad*

At the very moment the god would have me—
rescued, by river-magic, by the strong current
of a father's love, mid-stride, toes rooting in loam,
breasts barking over, my long hair leafing out
into wind-swept laurel. *Daphne*—even the syllables
of my name transformed into sunlight, into silence.
Beyond my grasp. Everything I ever loved.
One last scream— *Papa!* —and from now on,
to reach for you only with the frill of sallow blossoms,
pollen skimming the face of the stream.

2.   *Sculptor*

Even at twenty-five, I didn't need
a Prince of the Church to tell me: it was a masterpiece.
I delivered "Apollo and Daphne" to Borghese,
received the last of my thousand *scudi* in a velvet purse,
bowed respectfully, took my leave.

I knew what I'd done:
made stone *want*, the way gods want.
Made the girl's cry flood the Carrara.
Vanity, yes—that small apostrophe
of iron-oxide, visible on the bridge of her nose,
to remind them all: I could make even poor stone
bend to my will.

Then the years and the years. I've become the victim
of my own alchemy. I turned desire into marble,

marble into silver, silver into a palazzo, fine clothes,
and women who have no reason to flee.
Take pity on me, Lord—let me finish transforming
my heart into stone, before Hades has me.

Sund

> "What do I do?
> I show you barns in the air over Porter Creek.
> Tulips that drop from trees in Venezuela
> and fall to the ground
> bursting into roosters."
>
> —*Robert Sund*
> from: "Answering, for my Brother"

He was a young man training to be a doctor
at U. of Washington when he met Roethke who
cursed him with burgeoning vision and
anointed him with inky bliss. Quite a thing,
to overturn another man's purpose with beauty.
Sund thought it an almost-unrepayable debt.

Had he not built his shack in Ish River country—
–*ish*, the syllable of moving waters: Duwamish, Snohomish,
holy ground of the riverine valley, Puget Sound—
had he inhabited instead the hectic streets of Seattle,
he'd have been just another lunatic people steered clear of,
imagining the stink of whiskey on warm breath.

Instead, Sund spent his nights at a small lamplit table
serving tea to Basho, Rabbe Enckall, Su Tung-P'o, passing
from hand to hand the glass inkwell, sipping distilled darkness,
and laughing until it hurt. There is no accounting for the effect
one life has upon another—the neural rivers changing course.
Time collapses, and even the poets will tell you: it's all profit, all loss.

Greek Fragment

Surely the most beautiful of musics:
outstretched arms reaching for that
lost harp—blunt wrists, for the arched
marble fingertips poised above the strings—

and all longing for the courtyard of Alcaeus
where this stone musician shared his days.
Music, all of it—the fig trees and their fig-green light,
the black clutches of swaying grapes.

Politics, banished from this garden, along with
news from the capital, and the quiet commands
that send young men into war. An accumulation
of absences: harp, the harper's hands,

the shriek and clatter of battle, the cut-
and-dried verses to garland the graves,
and even the old kingdom itself, ground down
into that much more wind-swept sand.

Provence
    after Van Gogh's "Wheat Field with Reaper and Sun"

So many reapers appearing,
near the end, in wheat fields and yellow rape,
in mornings and evenings, the wind slicing
down from Les Apilles, the grain bowing,
the daubed man standing waist-deep in
ochre, in bristled spikes of citron, sienna,
his head a smear of umber and tourmaline,
flecked gaze of crimson, the sweeping scythe
of crow's wing, of storm edge and luminous
steel-blue sky, everything honed upon
the sun's whetstone, every brushstroke
the fate of the harvest, the smell of
linseed oil, cyan and cobalt
muddy on the tongue, working fast
in failing light, nearing the end, nearing
the horizon, the skyful, the awful,
billowing with bone and egg shell and zinc,
speared by cypress, licked by onyx, and
the daubed man looking up, alone in the fields
and the sheaves of wheat, armful after armful,
and the terrible weight of the yield.

Oracle

                Église Notre-Dame, Auvers-sur-Oise

When the priest raised the host full
moon through bare sycamore the bark
like scourged flesh *body of Christ* and as
one by one the mouths of the congregants
fell open crows too brazen to be silenced
by nightfall winter staking its claim *forever
and ever* candlelight quivering an oracle
inside every eye and in between an un-
leavened silence *eat this it is my body* now
gusts shake dew from cold branches *drink this
it is my blood* then a sudden eruption car door
or gunshot echoing through stone porticos as
all the black wings scatter across parched
fields but my mouth remains shut tight
barely breathing waiting for a sign for some
undeserved assurance even as I deny the very
possibility *do this in remembrance of me*

Poem Beginning with a Line from Bob Hicok

The night touches me, turns me to Braille.
Bare flesh is recitation. I am pierced
by punctuation. I might well be poetry.

I am nursed by epic hungers, blind fates.
The late winds read and re-read their
favorite passages. Song fills its own sails.

Maybe this is what we were dying for all along—
something dark and riddled with stars
that would commit us to memory.

The Arborist
(for Seamus Heaney)

With a two-handed grip,
plunging the steel wand deep, there

and again over there—the root web, he explains,
as broad as the dogwood's crown,

feeding the underworld so we here might. . .
all in good time. . ... Nutrients flood the ground while,

fortified, the winter-scarred branches
snatch at the failing summer sun.

∂

They buried you today in Derry.
. . .*beside the still waters* (if nothing else,

the soothing purl of sibilance).
...*for His Namesake* (as well as our own).

That the old text comforted you
is itself a comfort. But I am more relieved

by the gravelly syllables tumbled smooth
in the fluency of your voice—the familial

and the forgotten your poetry unearthed.
More than once it yanked me, despairing, up

from the bog, and back to the work at hand.
Ineluctable music—even with you gone:

the gruff sound you made cutting turf
with the nib of your pen—while

your father's fathers bent to their work,
writing verse with the tips of their spades.

The Song

*The song of the marsh wren divides the world
into two discreet* the marsh wren's song,
a small extravagance, a bright vessel filled and overfilled
with *the world into two*, into motion, into shameless praise,
hidden in the cattails, *the song*, the song, close
as breath and yet you stare *into two discreet*, into
the green rushes the wind weaves, re-weaves, and find no trace
of *the world into two discreet entities*: and in the lulls,
the eye moves cautiously through the dark chapels,
searching for a sign, a winking eye, a flickering wing,
this being, smaller than a finger, the white slash of its eyebrow,
the upswept tail, *the song of the marsh wren*, all rhythm,
all motion, wind off the pond top, the broad palms
of the lilies proffering beads of rain, the eye and ear
wedded to one desire—and when the bird begins again,
something small and sharp-beaked speaks
inside the rib cage, fills and overfills the breath, makes
its own version of melody, and the song, *the song of the marsh wren
divides the world into two discreet entities:
the sung and the unsung*—and just like that
you know what you've wanted, waited for,
just like that, all along.

From the Bridge
(for Sonny Rollins)

And then Sonny jumped from the bridge.
Clutching the swan-necked tenor.
The keys fluttering like moon
after cloud-fledged autumn moon.

The torrent of his plunge.
Gusts making melody. Melody
stringing together stars like prayer beads,
and then the black stars toppling from their staves.

We listened as if it were a raptor's cry,
a *cri de coeur*, a cry for mercy.
There is beauty in descent because
we are all of us, all the time, falling.

When Sonny struck the water, the dark world
opened at last. Ten thousand eighth notes
gashed like sparks, like air bubbles rising,
like applause.

Gold Boat

        The Broighter Hoard; County Derry

Hull, a hand's length of beaten gold.
Gold straw for mast and spar and,
both port and starboard, nine bright twigs
for oars. The artist's burnished craft—

unearthed by a plow blade near Limavady,
after twenty-one centuries becalmed. Time
might easily have crushed it for good—and yet. . .
Tonight, the moon's a currach, cupped

like my father's palm. Memory in its hold.
A word-hoard massed like stars.
Our vessel, large enough to carry a single
warm breath across the tideless dark—

yet small enough to ferry
all the names of the dead from
the providence of our saying
to the perdition of the said.

A Soul
(for Jane Hirshfield)

They call it a soul, it's not a soul, it's
the feeling in the hand, just so much
cardamom, so much thyme, how
the tongue knows to strike one syllable,
bend another, song and instrument one
and the same, how the current surges when
she, almost casually, makes music of my name,
makes urgency of the ordinary, her lips touching
here, or mine caressing there, the tide turning
rocks below us in the cove, turning the craggy
heart smooth as a stone the soul lifts in its hand,
had a soul a hand, and tosses far out into
the raveling, unraveling blue, they call it
a sea, it's not a sea, it's a soul.

We
(for my wife)

I walked with you along the sea beside the sea,
our bare feet disappearing beneath the sand below the sand.
Twig-legged plovers scattered before the plovers scattering before us,
their high-pitched squeaks and skreaks and anxious scurry.
We strode until we too shivered into multiplicity—
our was-is-will-be bleeding one into another. And even when we
clambered up dune upon wavering dune and, for a moment's moment,
sat still to gaze, we felt ourselves subsumed within the endless
succession: blue inside white-pleated undulant blue—
soul inside sun-anointed rippling soul.

Carcinoma

Our great good fortune:
they performed a caesarean

on my wife, extracted death
before it could come full-term.

We've given the fear up for adoption.
Thank goodness for the days after,

even throbbing with pain, for the day's
repudiation of ever-after.

Some mornings, I still place my lips
on that pale scar as one might

a crucifix. A believer now
in now's elasticity, I kiss

love's continuance, grief's
temporary reprieve.

Shadow Play

A gamelan of sea-thrum, surf-clang, and smooth stones
tumbled chockablock along the shoreline.
After sunset, strung across the horizon,
a procession of black puppet-clouds acting out
old mythologies against the illuminated scrim:
heroes evolving into herons and into dolphins leaping.
Gods morphing into sylphs, and then silken maidens
dancing beside a river, who become the twisting branches
of the banyan, until they coalesce into gods again
before the candlelit theater dims.

Remind me once more: what happened to the lovers?
Did they escape the flames? Embrace them?
Did they go on singing like the *coquí*, the mosquitoes,
those pearly-eyed thrashers, somewhere out in the dark?
We sip rum out on the deck, give evening our rapt attention
until the no-see-ums chase us in. Even still,
we'll carry these dramas with us into our separate sleep
where other hands will take control, make us
war, weep, dance, soar—our shadow-silhouettes
backlit by loneliness and the Caribbean moon.

Apple

Tonight's moon is a slice of apple—
the one piece that did not make it into the pie,
that rocked on the cutting board like a skiff
on a lake in the *old country* I knew only
from stories—and all the while, the silver blade
went on turning the other apples into pained smiles,
sacrificing themselves to the dark god
of appetite and longing. But this one slice—
my grandmother lifted it directly to my mouth—
and I remember being swallowed by sudden
understanding, feeling myself chest-deep inside
a kind of love I hadn't a word for at the time,
but do now: *apple* (those dark seeds inside the word)—
the ruddy skin, white flesh, sweet fruition
giving way to this perishing silence.

Escapement

Barefoot at the screen door, I watched:
my wife, my son, the blue car driving off,
his arm thrust through the far window,
a single wing beating, and then my own
small tick-tock of a wave in response, bye-bye.
And suddenly it was clear:
This is my life.　　The maple green
scumbled through wire mesh,
the June sky stirring, the sound
of car wheels hard on a corner, a horn, and then
no sound at all.　　*My life.*　　A quiet jubilance.
Even in its retreat, I could not
keep my eyes from it. And somewhere,
steel teeth on the escapement:
a notch, and no more.
Another incremental breath,
and no less.

Sabbath Rain

Four fat
        white petals
slipped from
        the dogwood and
pressed atop
        the feeder dome
like a skullcap while,
        perched beneath it,
a minion of black-
        capped chickadees
chant and sway,
        stirred by thawed hungers
and the sweep of May rain.
        Respectful, they too
cover their heads,
        these students of
the ordinary seed,
        the everyday holy.

A Story about the Moth

who took three mouthfuls from
the linen shroud of poor Lazarus—

Lazarus—whose father, I imagine, inconsolable, wept outside

in merciless sun and, though schooled by hard years,
he appealed to the Magician to undo what cannot be undone,

because he'd heard stories that claimed otherwise.

Yet when do we ever give ourselves over to a story?
Perhaps not until, engulfed by its unfolding, we feel our own life

being wholly rewritten and destined now—*once upon a time*—

for other hungry mouths. So when the stone door
of the tomb was rolled back and the moth, replenished,

was swept again into daylight, it was clear—

or so it was told to me—he had become something more
than himself: the psalm of larval yearning, the patriarch

of clay-colored wings whose lineage is among us still.

No, all this did not take place *just before the miracle occurred*—
this *was* the miracle.

Mending

She leaned forward, my mother,
and took it between her teeth—

this lie I'd told, this sin, this failing
of the flesh that was (it goes without saying)

her flesh as well, shamed now by my
flawed-heart-want-can't-help-myself—

and bit the thread in two, freeing up
her bright needle and leaving behind, see,

the mended tear in the knee of my blue
school trousers: *see*, she said (and she could,

couldn't she, right to the heart of her
love-stunned little boy), *good as new*.

Starbucks

I'm meeting my father here.
He died nearly thirty years before
a place like this ever existed.

For fifteen cents, he could enjoy
a mug of joe at The Busy Bee,
Burt and Dave's, The Parkway Diner—

but no, more likely I'd find him
dream-worn at his own kitchen table,
blue flannel robe, aura of forsythia,

pouring a fresh cup, cream, two sugars.
To an eight-year-old, the coffee smell
on his breath seemed intoxicating,

alluvial, a bitter intimacy.
Now I find a seat beside the window,
buy each of us a tall latte and

sit patiently, watching the corona
of our milky foam,
retreating.

Supermoon

(for George Adam Harper)

Not the fat mandala the meteorologists
were touting on the news but

a dime-sized jewel floating beneath us
in the pond's black skies which

my grandson, nearly two, snatches up
in his small fist. Opening it slowly—

convinced of what he possesses,
and by what he's possessed—

he offers me his wet palm.
I kiss the moon there.

Slainte

Three months dead and your poem
appears in the glossy mag. Below
the by-line, your years pried apart
with a paltry black hyphen.
In your honor, I crack a cold one—
ragged moonlit clouds frothing atop
a pint of midnight—and toast
to all our fermented spirits, lush
on the summer tongue, our sullen
eloquence, the cold glass weeping
inside the palm, because—and you'd be
the first to remind me—you can no longer
see, sip, taste, savor, nor honor with song
this starless June diminuendo.
I can. And do.

Grief's

1.
Pinned between the letters:
that ink-black eye weeping.

That fallen leaf from the ruined garden.
That placeholder for pure absence.

That flaw in an unblemished sky
that possessed me, utterly.

2.
After the bitterest of years—

my roster of heartbreak,

this wallow of longing—

after eviscerating shame
(and who more artful than I
with the chisel of blame,
quarrying my obdurate self?)—

after memory steeped in tears,

and after finally drinking my fill—

I can set the cup down now,
push back from the table,

and return to the day that's
always been waiting,

having loosened the hold of—
no, none of those lost faces—
but grief's apostrophe.

STEVEN RATINER

has previously published three chapbooks and been featured appeared in numerous anthologies; his work has appeared in scores of journals in America and abroad including Parnassus, Agni, Hanging Loose, Poet Lore, Salamander, QRLS (Singapore), HaMusach (Israel), and Poetry Australia. For several years, he was the poetry book critic for the Washington Post and, prior to that, The Christian Science Monitor. He's also written essays on poetry, literature and art for the San Francisco Chronicle, the Arrowsmith Journal, Horizon magazine, and Yankee Magazine. Giving Their Word – Conversations with Contemporary Poets was re-issued in a paperback edition (University of Massachusetts Press) and includes interviews with many of contemporary poetry's most important figures. In 2022, Ratiner completed his third term as the Poet Laureate for Arlington, Massachusetts. His Laureate project—the weekly Red Letter Poems—continue today and features a diverse range of poets, from up-and-coming talents to some of the most important voices from America and abroad. (steven.arlingtonlaureate@gmail.com). He was recently elected as the new President of the New England Poetry Club, one of America's oldest poetry associations.

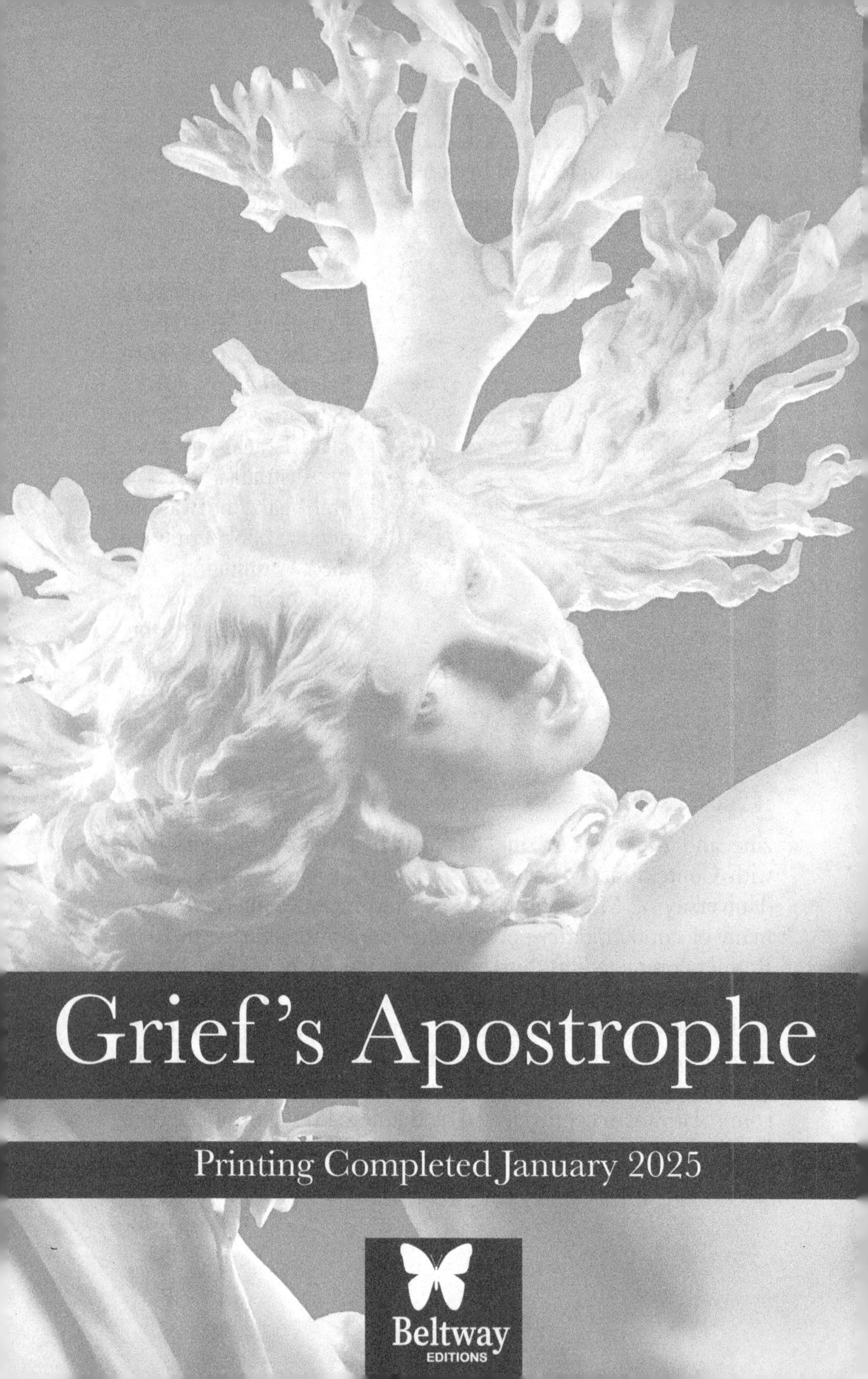

Grief's Apostrophe

Printing Completed January 2025